SUMMARY

Of

THE DIVINE EXCHANGE
The Sacrificial Death of the Cross

BENSON GERALD

Disclaimer

You are currently reading a SUMMARY of the Book titled ``The Divine Exchange: The Sacrificial Death of the Cross. The SUMMARY information is not ready to take the place of the original text, it serves as a complimentary guide to deepen the reader's comprehension. Once more, the goal of this book is to persuade readers to purchase the original work to deepen their grasp.

TABLE OF CONTENT

The Invitation

Jesus Christ has offered an invitation that extends to the whole human race: "Come
Please come to me, all ye tired and
I will relieve your burdens so you may relax "* No
regardless of your unique burden or
Regardless of the issue, God has a solution.
you.
But you can only find it in one spot.
The cross that Jesus died on is the answer.
It is by means of the cross, and only the cross.
—that you might get your supply
a solution to your issue, the information you
Let go of your load.

Expectantly read the following pages!

*Mat. 11:28, (NIV)

THE DIVINE EXCHANGE

The central theme of the gospel message is
centered on one particular historical event: the
Jesus' death on the cross was a sacrifice.
In regards to this, the author of Hebrews states:
"Because He [Jesus] made one offering (sacrifice).
has polished those who are being for all time.
sanctified" (Hebrews 10:14). (Hebrews 10:14). two strong
combinations of the words "perfected" and
"forever." They represent a sacrifice when combined.
which is aware of all of the needs of
the totality of humankind. Additionally, its results
extend into the future and throughout time
eternity.

Paul bases his ministry on this sacrifice.

Philippians 4:19 says: "Oh my God.
shall meet all of your needs in accordance with His
Christ Jesus' riches in splendor.
"All of Every aspect of your life, including

Your body, soul, mind, and your material and monetary
resources need.

Nothing is too big or too small to be covered by God's
provision. God's lone, sovereign act resulted in
together, every necessity and every hardship that
all of humankind at one dramatic moment.

God has not given us a lot of diverse
answers to the numerous issues of
mankind. Instead, He provides us with a single, complete
remedy that is His response to
every issue. We could have various different
backgrounds.
Despite our varied upbringing, we are all burdened.
with our own unique requirements, but to be given
God's solution is where we must all turn.
the same location—Jesus' cross.

The most thorough account of what happened
At the cross, success was awarded
700 years since the time of the prophet Isaiah.
even before it actually happened. In Isaiah\s53:10-11 the
prophet envisions a "righteous
Servant "whose soul was to be sacrificed

God as a sacrifice for sin. The creators of
all of the New Testament agree that

This unidentified "servant" is identified as Jesus.
The divine intent served by His

Isaiah 53:6 summarizes sacrifice:
We have all wandered like sheep, each going our own way, and the Lord has placed our collective guilt on Him.
Here is the fundamental issue that affects all of humanity: we have all chosen our own paths. Many of us have never engaged in specific sins like murder, adultery, robbery, and so forth.
However, there is one thing that unites us all: we each choose our own path. By doing this, we have disregarded God.

The Hebrew term Avon, here translated as "iniquity," best expresses this. Perhaps "rebellion"—against God, not against man—is the closest English word to this in modern usage.

But no single English word, be it "iniquity" or "rebellion," can really capture the essence of Avon. The word "Avon" is used in the Bible to refer to both iniquity and the retribution or bad results that iniquity brings with it.
For instance, in Genesis 4:13 Gain spoke these words in response to God's retribution for killing his brother:

The penalty is too severe for me to handle. The word "punishment" used here is Avon.

It addressed not just Cain's transgression but
Additionally, the punishment meted out to him.

Leviticus 16:22 talks about the scapegoat. The Lord was freed on the Day of Atonement. said: "The goat will carry all its burdens on itself." injustices committed in a remote area. That is Using symbolism, the goat carried more than just Israelite transgressions, as well as all humans the repercussions of their injustices.

Avon appears twice in Lamentations 4 with the same meaning. The phrase "penalty of the guilt of the daughter of my people" appears in verse 6. Verse 22 says it once more: "The retribution of your wickedness, O daughter of Zion." The phrase "the punishment of wickedness" is translated into each instance's single word, Avon. In other words, in its broadest sense, Avon refers to not only "iniquity," but also to all the bad results that iniquity brings about as a result of God's punishment.

This is relevant to Jesus' death on the cross. Jesus was sinless in and of Himself. The prophet declares in Isaiah 53:9, "He had
neither had He used force nor had He spoken with malice. However, he claims that "the LORD has thrown on Him the iniquity [avon] of us all" in verse 6. Jesus was not only identified with our sin, but He also suffered all of its negative effects. He removed them, much like the

scapegoat who had served as a type of Him so that they would never again fall upon us.

Herein lies the real significance and aim of the cross. A divinely preordained exchange occurred on it. Jesus first suffered in Considering all the negative effects that were owed to our sin as a result of divine justice.

God now provides us with all the good in return. that resulted from their pure submission to Jesus.

In a nutshell, Jesus experienced the bad that was owed to us so that we would get the good that was owed to him. Because Jesus previously bore the whole weight of the fair punishment owed to us for our transgressions, God can grant this to us without violating His own eternal justice.

The only source of all of this is the infinite grace of God, and it is purely by faith received.

There isn't a cause-and-effect argument that makes sense. None of us have ever done anything to merit such a proposal, and we will never be able to.

Scripture exposes numerous facets of the exchange as well as numerous contexts for its application. But in every instance, the same idea is true:

Jesus suffered harm so that we would get the corresponding benefit.

Isaiah 53:4-5 makes the first two components of the discussion clear:

He has undoubtedly suffered our sufferings and carried our illnesses, but we still thought of Him as being tormented and stricken by God.

The chastisement (suffering) for our peace was upon Him, and it is by His stripes (wounds) that we are healed.

However, He was wounded for our trespasses, and He was bruised for our iniquities.

Here, two realities are intertwined; one applies to the spiritual realm, the other to the physical. Jesus took the punishment we deserved for our sins and wrongdoings in

the spiritual realm so that we could be pardoned and find peace with God. Romans 5:1 is cited. Jesus took on our physical ailments and pains so that we could be healed by His wounds.

In two New Testament verses, the exchange's bodily applicability is affirmed. Isaiah 53:4 is referenced in Matthew 8:16–17, where it is stated that Jesus:

... cured everyone who was ill in order to make Isaiah the prophet's prophecy true:

"He Himself took our infirmities And bore our afflictions."

The apostle also makes reference to Isaiah 53:5–6 in 1 Peter 2:24 when he writes of Jesus:

... who Himself bore our sins in His own body on the cross, that we, having died to sins, may live for righteousness—by whose stripes [wounds] you were healed.

The two-way conversation outlined in the aforementioned verses can be summed up as follows:
Jesus endured punishment so that we could receive mercy.
Jesus suffered wounds so that we can recover.

Isaiah 53:10, which indicates that the Lord made the soul of Jesus "an offering for sin," reveals a third part of the exchange.

This needs to be understood in the context of the different sin-offering laws included in the Mosaic law. The offender was required to deliver his animal sacrifice to the priest, which could be a sheep, a goat, a bull, or another animal. Over the offering, he would confess his

transgression, and the priest would figuratively transfer the sin from the confessor to the offering.

The animal would then be put to death, paying the price for the transgression that had been committed.
shifted over to it.

All of this was planned in advance by God to serve as a prelude to the ultimate, all-sufficient sacrifice of Jesus. The sin of the entire world was transferred to Jesus' soul on the cross. In Isaiah 53:12, the consequence is stated: "He poured out His soul unto death."
Jesus atoned for the sin of the entire human race through His sacrificial, substitutionary death.

Paul makes reference to Isaiah 53:10 in 2 Corinthians 5:21 while also emphasizing the benefit of the exchange:

Because He [God] caused Jesus, who was sinless, to become sin for us, we might now become the righteousness of God in Him.

Paul is speaking about God's own righteousness—a righteousness that has never known sin—and not any kind of righteousness that we can acquire through our own efforts. No one among us will ever merit this.

It towers over our own righteousness just as much as heaven does over the earth. It can only be accepted via trust.

The following can be used to summarize the third element of the conversation:

For the sake of making us righteous with His righteousness, Jesus became sinful by taking on our wickedness.

The discussion's subsequent element follows naturally from the first. The Bible as a whole, both the Old and the New Testaments, emphasizes that death is the result of sin. The Lord declares in Ezekiel 18:4 that "The soul who sins shall die." The apostle claims in James 1:15 that "Sin, when it is fully matured, brings out death." It was only natural for Jesus to experience the death that results from sin once He came to identify with our sin.

In Hebrews 2:9, the author states that "Jesus... was made a little lower than the angels, for the suffering of death... that He, by the mercy of God, could taste death for everyone," which serves as further evidence of this. The death He experienced was an inescapable result of the human guilt He had accepted. He took on the sin of all people, and as a result, he experienced the punishment that all people deserved.

Jesus now extends the gift of eternal life to everyone who accepts His substitutionary offering. Paul contrasts these two options in Romans 6:23:

Because eternal life in Christ Jesus, our Lord, is God's [unmerited] gift to us rather than death, which is the wages of sin.

Therefore, the following might be said to sum up the fourth aspect of the exchange:

Jesus sacrificed His own life in order for us to obtain His.

Paul elaborates on another aspect of the exchange in 2 Corinthians 8:9:

Because you are aware of the grace of our Lord Jesus Christ, who, while being wealthy, became poor for your benefit so that you might become rich through His poverty.

The trade-off is obvious: from poverty to wealth. Jesus took on poverty so that we can have abundant life.

How did Jesus get into poverty? He was not poor throughout His earthly career, contrary to some people's perceptions. Even though He didn't carry much cash, He never went without anything.

They had nothing lacking when He dispatched His disciples on their own. Refer to Luke 22:35. So, far from being destitute, He and His disciples consistently gave to the needy. (Consider John 12:4–8 and 13:29.)

Money has the same worth whether it's taken out of a bank or a fish's mouth, despite the fact that Jesus' methods of doing so were occasionally unusual.

Referring to Matthew 17:27 His methods for supplying food was somewhat odd as well, but a guy who can feed 5,000 men (including women and children) a filling lunch is undoubtedly not poor by conventional standards! Matthew 14:15–21 is cited.

In actuality, Jesus perfectly embodied the biblical definition of "plenty" throughout His whole earthly career. He always had everything He required to carry out God's desire in His own life. In addition to all of this, He never ran out of things to give to other people.

When did Jesus start living in poverty for our sake? On the cross, is the response. Moses enumerated the four characteristics of utter poverty in Deuteronomy 28:48: hunger, thirst, nakedness, and need of all things. On the cross, Jesus went through all of this in its entirety.

He was famished. He hadn't eaten anything in almost 24 hours.

He was parched. It was one of His final words, "I thirst!" (John 19:28).

It was just him. His entire wardrobe had been stolen by the military (John 19:23).
All things were necessary for him. He was no longer the owner of anything. Following his passing, He was interred in a borrowed coffin and robe (Luke 23:50-53). As a result, Jesus absolutely and exactly suffered utter poverty for our sakes.

Paul expands on the benefit of the exchange in 2 Corinthians 9:8:

And God is able to make all grace abound in your direction so that you always have enough for everything and have a surplus for every good deed.

All throughout, Paul is careful to underline that God's grace is the only foundation for this exchange. You can never earn it. Only faith is capable of receiving it.

Our "plenty" will frequently resemble that of Jesus while He was on earth. We won't keep big sums of cash on hand or make sizable bank deposits. However, we will occasionally have enough for our own needs and extra for the needs of others.

The words of Jesus cited in Acts 20:35 provide a significant clue as to why this degree of provision is made: Giving brings more blessings than receiving.
God intends for every one of His children to be able to experience the larger blessing. He, therefore, gives us sufficient resources to meet our own needs and to give to others as well.

This exchange's fifth feature could be In summary:

Jesus endured our destitution.
In order for us to share His bounty.

The exchange that takes place at the cross also includes the emotional kinds of suffering that result from man's sin. Again, Jesus suffered the bad so that we could also

experience the good. Shame and rejection are two of the most heinous wounds inflicted upon us by our transgression. On the crucifixion, Jesus experienced both of them.

Shame can range in severity from a sharp sense of shame to a groaning sense of unworthiness that prevents a person from having a meaningful relationship with God or other people. One of the most frequent causes, which is on the rise in our modern culture, is any kind of childhood sexual abuse or molestation.

This frequently causes scars that can only be healed by God's grace.

The author of Hebrews states about Jesus' suffering on the crucifixion that He "endured the cross, despising the disgrace" (Hebrews 12:2).

The most abhorrent method of execution, designated for the lowest rung of criminals, was hanging.

The individual who would be put to death was stripped of all his clothes and stood nude in the street, humiliated and jeered by onlookers. Jesus was humiliated to this extent as He hung on the cross (Matthew 27:35-44).

God's goal is to share His eternal glory with people who put their faith in Him, replacing the disgrace that Jesus endured. The author of Hebrews 2:10 writes:

It was appropriate for God to make Jesus, the source of their salvation, flawless through suffering in order to bring many sons to glory.

All who put their faith in Jesus will be freed from their own guilt because of the disgrace that He experienced while he was crucified. Additionally, He then shares with us the glory that is His by right of eternity!

Another wound, often even more terrible than shame, exists. That's rejection.
This is typically the result of a failed relationship of some kind. It is initially brought on by parents who reject their own offspring. The rejection could be overt, expressed in harsh, negative ways, or it could just be a lack of acceptance and affection. If a pregnant mother harbors unfavorable thoughts towards the kid inside her womb, the child will likely be born feeling

rejected and this rejection may last into maturity or even until death.

Another typical reason for rejection is the dissolution of a marriage. The words of the Lord in Isaiah 54:6 give a clear picture of this:

"The LORD will bring you back as if you were a wife left and disturbed in spirit—a wife who married young, only to be rejected."

(NIV)

According to Matthew 27:46 and 50, which detail the height of Jesus' sorrow, God made a provision for the wound of rejection:

Around nine o'clock, Jesus called out in a piercing voice. "Eli, Eli, lama Sabachthani?" Specifically, "My God, My God, why have You abandoned Me?" After wailing loudly once more, Jesus finally gave His spirit up.

The Son of God cried out to His Father for the first time in the universe's history, yet there was no answer. Jesus identification with man's guilt was so complete that God's unwavering holiness led Him to reject even

His own Son. In this sense, Jesus suffered the most terrible kind of rejection: rejection from a father.

He passed very shortly after that, not from crucifixion wounds but rather from a broken heart brought on by rejection.

Immediately after, Matthew's account continues, "And lo, the curtain of the temple was rent in two from top to bottom."
Symbolically, this showed that a path had been made clear for fallen man to interact directly with a holy God.
Jesus' rejection paved the way for us to be welcomed as God's children. Paul summarizes this in Ephesians 1:5–6:

He [God] has made us accepted in the Beloved after 'having predestined us to adoption as sons by Jesus Christ to Himself."

(KJV)

Jesus was rejected, and as a result, we are accepted.

Never has the need for God's solution to humiliation and rejection been greater than it is now. According to my estimation, at least 25% of adults worldwide are still dealing with rejection or shame-related wounds.

My satisfaction in pointing such folks to the healing that comes from Jesus' cross has been immeasurable.

Following is a summary of the two emotional components of the encounter at the cross that have been analyzed:

Jesus took on our humiliation so that we could partake in His majesty.

Jesus put up with our rejection so that He may be accepted by the Father.

The exchange's components that were examined above touch on some of humanity's most fundamental and pressing needs, but they are by no means all-inclusive. In reality, there is no need brought about by man's rebellion that is not met by the same exchange principle:

Jesus suffered evil in order that good can be delivered to us. This idea unlocks God's provision for all of our needs once we learn to put it into practice in our daily lives.

One more, dramatic element of the conversation is left, as Paul explains in Galatians 3:13–14:

Because it is stated, "Cursed is everyone who hangs on a tree," Christ became a curse for us in order to rescue us from the curse of the law and grant the blessing of Abraham to the Gentiles in Christ Jesus, enabling us to receive the promise of the Spirit through faith.

The rule of Moses, as stated in Deuteronomy 21:23, states that a person executed by hanging on a "tree" (a wooden gibbet) consequently came under the curse of God. Paul applies this law to Jesus on the cross. He then draws attention to the outcome's opposite: the blessing.

This component of the dialogue can be examined without needing to be a theologian:

Jesus became a curse so that we could become blessed.
The term "the curse of the law" refers to the curse that befell Jesus. Moses provided a comprehensive list of both the blessings and the curses associated with following the

law in Deuteronomy 28. Deuteronomy 28:15–68's litany of curses can be summed up as follows:

- Embarrassment
- Barrenness
- Unfruitfulness
- Bodily and mental illness
- Family dissolution
- Poverty
- Defeat
- Oppression
- Failure
- God's disfavor

Do some of these phrases describe some aspects of your life? Do certain things cast a foreboding shade over you, blocking the sunshine of God's blessing that you so desperately want? If so, it's possible that a curse—from which you need to be freed—is the primary source of your issues.

Try to visualize Jesus as He hung there on the cross to understand the full agony of the curse that befell Him.

One of Jesus' disciples had betrayed Him, and the remainder had deserted Him (though some subsequently came back to witness His suffering at the hands of the authorities). Jesus had been rejected by His own countrymen. He was hanging

naked between the ground and the sky. His spirit was burdened by the sin of all humanity, and his body was torn by the agony of countless wounds. He had

been rejected by Earth, and heaven had not heard His cries.

His vital stream ebbed out onto the hard, dusty ground as the sun withdrew its brightness and night enveloped Him. But right as He passed away, alone, a victorious cry erupted from the shadows: "It is accomplished!"

The phrase "It is finished" is merely one word in the Greek original. The word in question is in the perfect tense, which implies "to make anything entire or perfect." It might be translated as "It is entirely perfect" or "It is completely complete" in English.

Every negative effect that human rebellion had on the world has been taken on by Jesus. He had experienced every punishment for breaking God's commandments. All of this was done so that we can also benefit from all of His obedience's blessings. Such a sacrifice is astounding in scale but amazing in execution.

Have you been able to embrace this story of Jesus' death and everything He won for you with faith? Are you currently eager to receive God's complete provision?

There is one obstacle that each of us must overcome: the obstacle of unforgiving sin. Do you already know for sure that Jesus' sacrifice has resulted in your sins being pardoned? If not, you should start there.

You might simply pray:

"God, I own that I am a sinner and that there is unforgiving sin in my life." Please pardon all of my transgressions in the name of Jesus, as I firmly believe that Jesus suffered punishment so that I can get forgiveness.

According to God's Word, "If we confess our sins, He is faithful and righteous to forgive us our sins and to purify us from all unrighteousness"

(1 John 1:9). Believe what God says! Believe that He has already pardoned all of your sins right now!
You just need to respond in one way, and that one way is the only way that true faith can be expressed. To express gratitude, please!

Take action right away! Say, "I'm grateful. Lord Jesus thank You for being punished so that I could be pardoned. Although I don't entirely comprehend, I do believe and I am glad!"

You now have access to all the kingdoms of God because sin has been removed as a barrier.

God has provided through the cross.
Each one must be received by simple faith in God's Word, just as the forgiveness of sin.

Each of us has unique requirements, and
must individually approach God to receive His
provision. Here is a sample of broad language.
that you may utilize to claim any other
provisions outlined in this manual.
Dear Jesus, I appreciate that you were
to be healed, I must be injured.

'm grateful, Lord Jesus, that you became sinful through my sinfulness so that You could become righteous through mine.

'm grateful that You died for me, Lord Jesus so that I can have Your life.

Thank You, Lord Jesus, for bearing with my need so that I can share in Your riches.

Dear Jesus, I'm grateful that You took on my humiliation so I may partake in Your glory.

Dear Jesus, I appreciate that You endured my rejection instead of me.

Your approval from the Father.

Lord Jesus, I'm grateful You were made a curse so I may receive a blessing.

Each answer to your prayers has progressed. God's power has been released into your life through your initial prayer.

However, that is just the beginning.

You must complete the following three steps in order to appropriate the entire provision you desire:

1. Examine the Bible for yourself to confirm these realities.

2. Constantly reiterate the specific exchange detail that satisfies your demand.

3. Continue to thank God for His blessings as a way of reinforcing your faith.
You'll believe God's actions on your behalf more the more you give Him thanks. And the more you trust in Him, the more you'll desire to give Him thanks.

These two actions—thanking and believing, believing and thanking—are like a staircase that will lead you higher and higher into the fullness of God's provision.

The Exchange Made At The Cross

Every act of God's mercy has one and only one sufficient foundation: the exchange that took place on the cross. Jesus endured punishment so that we could receive mercy.

Jesus suffered wounds so that we can recover.

For the sake of making us righteous with His righteousness, Jesus became sinful by taking on our wickedness.

Jesus sacrificed His own life in order for us to obtain His.

Jesus suffered because of our need so that we could spread His plenty.

Jesus took on our humiliation so that we could partake in His majesty.

Jesus put up with our rejection so that He may be accepted by the Father.
Jesus became a curse so that we could become blessed.

Final Summary

This is not a comprehensive list. There are further facets of the deal that may be mentioned. But each of them represents a unique aspect of the provision God has created through the death of Jesus. The Bible encapsulates them in one big, all-encompassing word: salvation. Christians frequently restrict the experience of salvation to being born again and having one's sins forgiven. Despite how wonderful this is, it just represents the beginning of the whole salvation that the New Testament reveals.

`` "All you need" refers to all aspects of your life:
Body
Mind
Emotions
Material need
Soul
Financial need
Discover how to apply the divine Exchange to your own life.

Made in the USA
Columbia, SC
13 November 2023

26153942R00020